15 Minutes with My Father

Tom Zegan

ISBN: 979-8-90118-738-8

www.15MinutesWithMyFather.info

1 John 4:4

Greater is he that is in you than he that is in the world.

Foreword

When I was young, I didn't think much about death. My Grandparents seemed like constants, always there at the family gatherings, especially at the pool parties and BBQs we would have at their house in Northridge, CA. I remember my Grandpa always telling us bible stories, and we'd always laugh at his jokes, even though they weren't that funny. My fondest memories were watching my Grandpa teach us at ***"Christian Youth in Action,"*** which was held every summer in Riverside, CA. At California Baptist University. It was there that I first accepted Jesus into my heart when I was only four years old. It was such an honor to later be able to attend ***"Christian Youth in Action"*** when I finally became a teenager. It was there that I actually learned from my Grandpa how to lead someone to Christ.

But life has a way of teaching you how precious time really is. I was with my grandfather when he took his last breath. It's a moment in time that will never leave me. There's a kind of sacred silence that fell in the room, where the ordinary world seems to pause and eternity brushes up against you. I remember holding his hand, looking at his face and realizing in that instant how much he meant to me, not just as my grandfather, but as a man filled with God's love who shaped my family and who also shaped me.

That moment has stayed with me and it is why this book that my dad wrote, ***"15 Minutes with My Father,"*** is so important to me. It isn't just my dad's story, it's our family's

story. A son speaking to his father, a grandson remembering his grandfather and all of us wondering what lies beyond this life.

In these pages, my dad has written the conversation we all wish we could have had with those we've lost. He imagines my grandfather returning, not as a ghost, but as a gift from God. Fifteen minutes to share what heaven is like, what eternity means and what really matters in the end. Reading it, I heard my grandpa's voice again. I saw his smile. I remembered the way he encouraged us as teenagers, the way he taught us the bible, the way he showed God's everlasting love.

This book is more than just words on paper, it's a bridge. A bridge between the living and the departed, between generations, between heaven and earth. My hope is that as you read it, you will feel what I felt: peace, comfort and the reminder that God's love is stronger than death.

"For me, this book is not just about what my grandfather said in those imagined fifteen minutes. It's about what he left us with in real life: faith, love and the courage to keep believing. To love unconditionally those around us.

I will never forget being with him the day he crossed over into eternity. But I will also never forget the life he lived, the legacy he left and the hope he has given all of us. ***"15 Minutes with My Father"*** is a reflection of that legacy.

I am so proud to be his "*favorite*" grandson and proud to stand between the generations as we remember him. May his words in these pages bless you as much as his life blessed me."

Michael Addison – Grandson

Dedication

This book is dedicated to my father, who was my greatest example of the most Godly man I've ever known. Not only did he talk the talk, but he walked the walk every day of his life until the last day of his life. My prayer is that I can live a Godly life similar to the one that my father lived. I'm so glad that he was my father, and I know that I will someday see him again in heaven.

I'd like to thank all of those who helped make this book possible, especially my mother, who was always there by my father's side, my son Addison, who has such a strong love for his grandfather, and my best friend Dan, who encouraged me to keep writing.

Tom Zegan – Son

Biography

My father was born in Chicago on January 10, 1938 during the end of the great depression. He was raised in a time of great challenges and as well as great hope. When he was only six years old, his father was drafted into the army to fight in World War II. My grandfather was on a boat on his way to the Philippines on August 6 & 9, 1945, the day that the atom bomb was set off over Hiroshima and Nagasaki, Japan.

My dad grew into a man marked by resilience, faith and compassion for God's kingdom. From an early age, he had the desire to serve the Lord as an altar boy at his local Church. My dad displayed a natural warmth that drew people to him, especially young people, who found in him not only a mentor but a warm and genuine friend.

At the age of 18, my dad married my mom, and they were married up until his death for just under 68 years.

Throughout his adult life, my dad was a man of service, whether to his family or his Christian ministry. He dedicated his life to serving Christ through working for ***"Child Evangelism Fellowship"*** for 42 years. With the goal to lead children to Christ. He worked hard, providing for those he loved, but his true legacy was not measured in possessions or titles. It was measured in the countless lives he touched with the Gospel of Christ.

RELIGION

Bible study shows book for more than Sunday

BY STARR SPENCER

, NORTHBRIDGE—Members of San Fernahdo Valley Chilstlans advzzate lor paty TV Ea kic study wraung holding in "rai alible stado.

Calied ' Five:Day Cluns, grouge nost for on mitites for five consecult werk days and also to help them daily Bibls study '

Mary gegan caim to resech children who use Summres to svim and play in lscd parks fiom the sreeted, notunteers.

"Tivie 1ids don't rEach me Brble more han :'ll:te br oil pundays and also to help thear dally. "

San Fernando Valley Ch-Fisitare advocate for dallV Bible study amens crill-

hten thaul ..lise ongraced for dally Mernbers doyingthe've 'eckde 'an ths hone of screened volunrliers-

'Mary kids-don't read-the bibir the dont aftent church' wheri theroacks.

Pui;Day Club, scri.ccastonaily vena reefach weak ime in homes of scessened to Stevesloonk Rap.

The Worlds Mas 100 tf is programinfy odunreers like Trudy Affolter coordinating.

Edmond says, "20ift lat c tench children who dim autlend church grounds wnone requested by parents.

the Northridgr office coordinating in Northtinge: vine's rcours es Beheeen Laoa 1500, 5 weekeraenation in home of screnned.

"We doot do a lot of advertisilig,"' Chancligs. donare $100 in spensor a clull in hovember

Flu day Llubs ored groud that tif rench six churcher weekis. Wi ithe bepl them of ailjer.

who dort take par tin saying exetrly what i meng 'or righe.'

"Tros: day cltubs ive a gpict by lraaner that hotl. vhen the, aith maucaf to grepes, and stantin, skth as hebsaia Loper and led

groups are improbon respectures a, Samevhu calli svrlan. but 5wo for chuech in ccent ve state sunt date-fun sge

"Hare ran acminaria of volunteers, that tos the same age crcun do school weetts." we E3(groope tine the invit 5bo, Novcrsinliy:n bradio telf for Bible, hrw alst mrp or the chikiren.

"We dcn't lut., a: Tiban say ssactly wi Idig ai'that stork tair Joncln to1 charelt in'i ceol vears baid..

They specify the anir allowing ch lubcr ci pardi sin, probert and scharurc in recean yeats," therm

His gift of teaching children about Christ became a defining theme of his life. He was a teacher to other teachers, and he taught his teachers, he guided them and believed in their potential, through programs like "Christian Youth in Action," "Good News Clubs," "5 Day Clubs," and "Camp Good News." He was always quick to encourage his students and teachers and slow to criticize. To his own family, he was a source of steady love and practical wisdom. To his community of faith, he was a figure of wisdom and strength. Both he and my mom started one of the first "Awana Clubs" in California at Nyeland Community Church in Oxnard, CA.

He carried with him the values of honesty, perseverance and his Christian faith. He believed in working hard, living simply and showing Gods love to those around him. Though life brought its share of trials, my dad met them with courage and humility.

After his passing, those who knew him often recalled his smile, his patient guidance, and his unshakable belief in his creator. His memory continues to inspire those he left behind, reminding them to live with compassion and purpose every day in Christ Jesus.

My father lived for eighty-six years; his life spanned over decades of history, change, and growth. But through it all, he remained steady, a man rooted in love, faith and family.

His story is not just one of years lived, but of lives changed. On March 25, 2024 my dad passed away at 86 years old in his home in Northridge, California with my mom and my son by his side.

Table of Contents

The Arrival

It was late evening and the house was quiet except for the low hum of the refrigerator in the kitchen. Outside, the Santa Ana winds blew through the branches of our navel orange trees, its rhythm a sound I had grown used to since my parents moved there. It was March 25th, exactly one year since my father had passed away.

Anniversaries of death are strange things. They do not arrive like birthdays or holidays, with balloons, cakes and music. They creep in quietly, waiting for you to notice the weight in your chest, the hollow in your day. I had been carrying that weight since his memorial service. Everywhere I went, drinking coffee, walking through the store, sitting in the living room, I felt his absence more sharply than on any other day.

I sat alone in the living room of my parents house, a photo album open across my lap. The light of a single lamp spilled onto the pictures, Dad standing with us as kids at Camp Good News, Dad holding a fishing pole while deep sea fishing, Dad laughing with a group of Awana kids from church enjoying the snow up in the mountains for the first time. His smile seemed so alive that my chest tightened.

That was when the air in the room shifted.

At first, I thought it was only the wind pressing against the window. But then I felt it again, an unmistakable warmth, as though someone had stepped just behind me, watching, present. The air grew heavier yet strangely comforting.

I closed the album slowly and looked up.

There he was.

Not in the way I had imagined when I dreamed or reminisced. Not a faded ghost or shadow. But my father stood there across the room, his figure outlined in a soft, golden light, as though heaven itself had stitched him together from memory and spirit. His face was different, he was much younger, like I remembered him in pictures when he was much younger, his eyes kind, his lips curled into that familiar half smile.

“Dad?” My voice cracked, caught between disbelief and longing.

"Yes, Son." His voice was strong and warm, the same voice that had once told bedtime stories and given me advice over the phone. "It's me, dad."

I froze, my mind scrambling for some sort of sense. "How is this even possible."

He lifted a hand in a calming gesture. "I don't have much time. Just a few minutes. God has allowed me to come back, to speak with you tonight on the anniversary of my death, because I know your heart has been heavy. Because in your mind you have been asking questions and searching for answers."

The weight of his words sank deep into me. My heart pounded, torn between skepticism and the overwhelming desire to believe. I stood slowly, my hands trembling.

"But you look so young," I whispered.

He chuckled softly. "Yea, I'm able to choose the age I want to look like."

I wanted to rush forward and embrace him, but something inside me hesitated. Perhaps it was reverence or perhaps fear that he might vanish if I reached out to touch him. Instead, I simply stared, memorizing every detail. He had hair that fell slightly over his forehead, like he had as a teenager.

"You look great," I said, a nervous laugh escaping.

"Better than the last time you saw me," he said with a grin. Yea, I remember saying goodbye for the last time right before he died and crying knowing that I would probably never see him alive again.

Tears stung my eyes. "Dad, I've missed you so much."

"And I've missed you too, son. More than you know. But missing isn't the same in heaven. It doesn't hurt the way it does down here. I can always check on you and see how you're doing."

I swallowed hard, words tumbling out before I could stop them. "Is it real then? Heaven and all of that?"

He nodded, his eyes glowing with an otherworldly certainty. "It's real. More real than this world. And I've come to tell you what it's like and what comes after you die. I want you to know, so you can live with confidence, not in fear or doubt."

I sank back into the couch, my hands pressed against my knees as if to steady myself. He moved closer, the golden light around him shifting with every step. Though his feet didn't quite seem to touch the floor, his presence was solid, undeniable. It wasn't a dream or a hallucination, it was real.

"Why me?" I asked. "Why now?"

"Because of all my children, you've carried my memory the deepest," he said. "Because tonight you sat with those memories and you thought a prayer and you didn't even realize it was a prayer, but I heard you. You asked, 'Where are you, Dad? What is it like?' And heaven heard. God listens, even in the quietest times."

The tears finally slipped free, rolling down my cheeks. I nodded slowly, unable to speak.

He sat down in his favorite armchair across from me, his movements natural, as though he had never left this earth. “I have so much to tell you and not much time. About heaven. About children. About what happens after you die and why people return. About hell, too, because you need to understand both. Not as myths or Sunday school stories, but as real places of the soul.”

I drew in a shaky breath. “I don’t even know where to start.”

He leaned forward, elbows on his knees, eyes locking with mine. “Start with your heart, son. What question burns deepest there?”

“Well first dad, you look great, why do you look so young?”

He said, “Son, heaven is filled with God’s glory and what you are seeing is just a manifestation of God’s glory.” Yea, but you have hair now, I’ve never see you with hair before except in old black and white pictures.

“That’s simple” he said, “In heaven we can choose to look whatever age we were in the past.

So I choose to look like I did when I met your mom in High School."

"So there are no ugly people in heaven?" My dad let out a laugh, "Not really," my dad said. "Heaven is the most perfect place and everyone in Heaven will look their best for God."

"I really just want to know if you're okay. That you're… happy."

His smile softened. "Oh, I am more than okay. In heaven, there's no pain, no sickness, no regret. Only peace and joy. But it's not just floating on clouds; it's a purpose. I still work with children, teaching, guiding, answering their questions as well as telling them many of the classic Bible stories from the Old Testament as well as stories about Jesus. While helping them grow in ways they weren't able to while their time was cut short on earth. In Heaven, every soul has a role and mine is still to teach and to guide the little children to the Gospel of Christ. That hasn't changed."

Something in me relaxed, a knot loosening after a year of tension. "So you're still… you?"

"Yes, I'm still me but better. Whole. Closer to what God intended me to be. In heaven, we're not stripped of who we are; we're fulfilled, completed. We are the best parts of ourselves, purified and perfected."

The grandfather clock in the living room ticked loudly, each second a reminder that this miracle was brief. But for that moment, time felt suspended, stretched wide to hold us both.

"I'll explain more," he said gently. "About the cycles of life, the waiting, the reasons some souls return sooner than others. But I need you to listen, truly listen. What I share will change how you see everything. It's not how we were taught as children."

I nodded, wiping my eyes. "I'm listening, Dad."

Crossing Over

The room grew still as I asked him the question that had lingered in my heart since the day he died.

"Dad," I whispered, "what was it like... when your soul left your body? What do you remember about dying? About crossing over?"

His eyes softened and for a moment the glow around him seemed to ripple with something deeper, like a memory carried in light. He leaned forward, resting his hands together and spoke with a voice both tender and steady.

"Son, death is not what most people imagine. We fear it because we think it is darkness or pain or a cruel ending. But it was none of those things. For me, it was a release. Like setting down a heavy burden I had carried for too long. My body was tired and worn out, every breath labored and I could feel the weight of years pressing down on me. But when the moment came, I slipped free of my body as easily as stepping out of some old clothes. I was lighter than I had ever been."

I swallowed hard, listening as though my soul itself depended on his words.

"I remember that very last breath," he continued, his eyes distant now as though he could still see it. "It was slow, shallow. I heard the voices of those around me, your mom and your son Addison, the quiet conversations whispered in the room. And then… I let go. Not with fear, not with struggle, just a quiet surrender. And the instant I did, the pain was gone. The weight vanished. My body lay there still, but I was not in it anymore. I could see myself just lying there, eyes closed, lifeless."

"I looked back, for just a moment. I saw your mom holding my hand. I saw the sadness in her eyes. I wanted to tell her I was OK and that I was still there, still alive, but the words wouldn't pass my lips. I could see your son Addison there trying to comfort his grandma. I heard him tell her that I was gone. All I could do was feel the love in the room, that love carried me forward. It was like a bridge between me and heaven."

His voice grew softer, reverent. "The next thing I knew, there was a bright light. Not a light from a lamp or the sun, but a light that seemed to come from everywhere and everything. Warm, gentle, embracing. It wasn't blinding, it was welcoming. Imagine the feeling of dawn breaking after a long, cold night. That's what it felt like. Peace washed over me, deeper than anything I had ever known. No fear. No regret. Just pure love."

I sat frozen, every word engraving itself on my heart.

"It felt," he went on, "like walking through a doorway I had always known was there but had never dared to open it. One moment I was in the living room with your mom and your son, and the next moment I was standing at the threshold of eternity. My body had fallen away, but I was still me, more me than I had ever been. My thoughts were clearer, my senses were sharper, my spirit was whole."

I drew in a shaky breath. "Was anyone there to greet you? Did you see… anyone?"

He smiled, his eyes glowing. "Yes, angels. Not with wings and harps as most people imagine, but beings of light, strong and gentle at the same time. They didn't speak with words, but I could understand them perfectly. Their presence filled me with calm and though no words were spoken, I heard them in my heart: *'You are going home now.'*"

My chest tightened, a mix of grief and awe.

"And then," he said, his voice trembling with joy, "I saw others. Faces I had not seen in years. Family. Friends. Souls who had died before me. They stood in that light, welcoming me, smiling with a joy that cannot be described. It was a homecoming. Not a death. A birth into something greater than life."

I pressed my palms together, my eyes stinging. "And you weren't afraid?"

He shook his head slowly. "Not for a moment. Fear belongs to the living. Once the soul is free, there is only peace. You don't cling to the body, you rejoice to be free of it. I thought leaving would be hard, but it was easier than falling asleep. The real miracle was waking up on the other side."

Silence filled the room for a moment, broken only by the steady ticking of the Grandfather clock we had bought my father for Christmas a few years ago.

"Dad," I whispered, "what did it feel like, that first step into eternity?"

He closed his eyes briefly, as if reliving it. "It felt like breathing for the very first time, like my lungs filled with something more than air, with light, with love itself. Every part of me came alive. My vision, my hearing, my very being was flooded with God's presence. It was overwhelming, yet gentle. I knew instantly, I was home."

I could hardly speak, tears slipping freely down my face.

He leaned forward, his gaze piercing mine. "So don't fear death, son. When your time comes, it won't be darkness, it will be dawn. It will not be the end, it will be the beginning of your truest life. You will step through that doorway and you will know what I now know:

love is all that remains. Love carries you. Love welcomes you. Love never ends."

The glow around him pulsed gently, as though heaven itself had whispered amen.

I sat there trembling, my heart torn open, but for the first time since his death, I felt the grip of fear loosen. I understood, not fully, but enough. My father had not been taken by death. But he had been welcomed into eternity.

What is Heaven Like?

The room was still bathed in that strange golden glow. Though I could see the lamp still shining on the end table next to me, its light seemed weak compared to the radiance surrounding my father. He leaned forward, elbows on his knees and gave me that look I knew so well, the look he used to give when he was about to tell me something important, something he wanted me to carry with me.

"You asked if I'm okay," he said softly. "But I want you to understand more than that. I want you to see heaven through my eyes, at least for a moment. It's not what most people picture. Not harps and endless singing, not a bland paradise where nothing ever changes. Heaven is alive."

"Alive?" I spoke.

He nodded. "More alive than here on earth. Here, we get tired and life is fragile, our bodies wear down, our hearts break, the years slip through our fingers. In heaven, life is fuller. Every sense, every feeling, every moment is sharper, brighter. Imagine the way the world looks after a heavy rain, the air clean, the colors deeper, the earth refreshed. That's how every day feels in heaven, all the time. It's like stepping into the truest version of reality."

I closed my eyes for a moment, trying to picture it. But my imagination faltered, limited only by earthly memories.

He continued. "There are fields and beautiful gardens, mountains and rivers, but they are more than landscapes, they're alive with God's glory. With meaning, every blade of grass seems to sing out to God, every drop of water reflects His presence. You don't just see beauty, you experience it, you become it."

This was so hard for me to comprehend, my mind couldn't even begin to phantom the complexity of what Heaven is truly like.

A smile tugged at his lips as he added, "And the children, son, the children are everywhere. Some who left earth too soon, some who were never even given the chance to be born. They're cared for, nurtured, and loved. I work with them every day."

I leaned forward. "That's what you do there? You work with children like you did here on earth?"

He nodded, his eyes brightening. "Yes. Just as I did here, but even more so. In heaven, every soul has a calling. Mine is to guide little ones and to teach them God's love and to show them the goodness of God. Imagine an endless playground, but one filled with laughter that heals, games that teach truth, and stories that shape eternity. The children are never lost, they're found, and we help them grow until their souls are ready for what's next."

My throat tightened. "So they're not alone?"

"No, never, no child is ever alone in heaven. Not the ones taken by illness, not the ones lost during childbirth or stillborn, and not the ones abandoned. Each is held, taught and cherished. That's part of what makes heaven so perfect, every soul belongs."

I felt my chest ache with both grief and comfort. "Dad… I always wondered about that. About the babies. About the kids who never got the chance, those that were stillborn or aborted."

He reached out, his hand hovering just above mine, not quite touching, but close enough that warmth spread through me. "They're safe, son. You can trust that was God's plan. Remember God knows all and He's not going to put a soul into a baby that isn't going to be born?"

"You mean like an aborted baby?" My dad smiled and said, "Exactly, and stillborn babies are babies that are born without a soul."

The words wrapped around me like a blanket. I hadn't realized how much I needed to hear them since my wife and I had aborted our first child many years ago.

He leaned back slightly, his gaze drifting as though he could see beyond the walls of the room. "There's more, though. Heaven isn't idle. Souls don't just sit in rest forever. There is music, yes, lots of music and worship too, awesome worship that fills our very beings with joy. My dad remembered how much I enjoyed leading worship, especially at Child Evangelism Fellowships' ***"Christian Youth in Action."*** But there's also work, meaningful work. We learn, we create, we help prepare others who will one day re-enter earth. We grow closer to God and in doing so, we become more and more of our true selves that were meant to glorify God. The best parts of who we were on earth are amplified in heaven. It's… fulfilling, in the way earth can only hint at."

"Do you see everyone again?" I asked, my voice tentative.

"Not all at once. Heaven is vast, greater than you can imagine. Souls are reunited, but also guided into what they need most. For some, that means healing. For others, learning and, yes, there are reunions, glorious reunions. I've seen old friends from ministry, family members, your Grandpa and Grandma and may of our relatives. But it's not like one great crowd. It's more… organized. Intentional, God places you where you belong, where you need to be."

I tried to process that. It was different than what I had pictured growing up and hearing in

Sunday School, different, but in many ways, but more comforting.

"And what about God?" I asked quietly. "Do you… see Him?"

My father's expression softened, reverence flickering in his eyes. "Not in the way you might imagine. God's presence is everywhere, like light, like music, like love itself. You can't escape it and you wouldn't want to. It fills you, sustains you, it completes you. Sometimes, souls are given glimpses of His glory more directly and when that happens… words fail. Even now, I can't explain it. But believe me, son, being in His presence is the greatest joy there is. I know that someday you and I will experience it together."

The golden glow around him pulsed gently, as if echoing his words.

"You don't long for earth?" I asked.

He smiled faintly. "Not the way you think. In heaven, we don't ache for what we've lost. But we do remember, with love, our times here on earth. We look back with gratitude, not sorrow. I remember the good times, the laughter, the love, the lessons, the people. And I look forward to the day when my family will be here with me. Time feels different here. Waiting isn't painful. It's patient, like a seed resting in the soil before it grows and eventually blooms."

His words sank deep, reshaping my understanding. For the first time since his death, I felt a sense of peace, fragile but real.

"But," he said, his voice lowering, "heaven is not the only place where souls go."

I felt the room grow slightly heavier at those words, though the glow remained.

"You mean hell," I said.

"Yes. And you must understand both to see the whole picture. Heaven and hell are not just symbols, not just stories told to scare us or comfort us. They are real places for the soul. And they are not final, they are part of the soul's journey. What you do on earth shapes where you go, but every soul continues on a path, whether in light or in darkness."

I swallowed hard, unsure if I wanted to hear the rest, yet knowing I had to know.

He leaned closer again, his eyes steady on mine. “In heaven, you find rest, peace, joy and growth. In hell… you face what you’ve done in the past. But I’ll explain that fully soon. For now, remember this: heaven is not just a reward; it’s a preparation, a resting place. It shapes souls for what’s to come next. It’s shaping me, and it will shape you one day too.”

The grandfather clock in the living room ticked louder, reminding me again of time’s relentless march forward. But for that moment, as he spoke, I felt as if eternity had opened just a crack, giving me a glimpse of something beyond my comprehension.

And I clung to every word.

Being Born Again

For a moment after he spoke of heaven's purpose, silence hung in the room. The grandfather clock in the living room faintly ticked, steady and indifferent, while the golden glow around my father seemed to breathe with him, pulsing gently as though it were alive too.

"Reincarnation," he said. Something I know that my dad didn't believe in when he was alive. But yet his tone both gentle, firm and filled with confidence. "It's one of the most misunderstood mysteries about the soul. Many deny it outright. Others imagine it wrongly, thinking it's random or cruel or that we are doomed to repeat life endlessly and without meaning. But the truth is far more ordered, far more filled with understanding, with love and mercy."

I leaned forward, my fingers clasped tightly together. "So it's real? Are we really born again?"

"Yes, eventually," he said, nodding slowly. "Every soul is given more than one life on this earth. How many lifetimes depends on the lessons needed to be learned and the growth needed to be made. Earth is a school. Heaven and hell are also classrooms, but earth is where the real testing and the practical application actually happen. That's where choices matter most, because earth is where free will runs wildest."

I tried to absorb his words. "Then why do some people live long lives, while others only a few years?"

"Because the length of one's life does not equal the depth of their lesson," he said simply. "A soul may only need a few short years to complete what it came to do. Another may need eighty or ninety. years What matters is not the number of years, but what the soul gains and gives in that time. Remember that our lives here on earth are just a vapor compared to eternity."

I nodded slowly, though my chest still tightened at the thought of those who had gone too soon.

"But here is the part most people don't understand," he continued, his eyes glowing with intensity. "After each lifetime, a soul enters either heaven or hell, for a period of rest, reflection and cleansing. And the length of that waiting time is tied to the number of years lived here on earth. If you live forty years on earth, you will wait forty years in heaven or hell before returning. If you live to be seventy, you will wait seventy years in heaven give or take a few years. Our time on earth determines how long we will remain in heaven or hell. That balance keeps the soul aligned with the rhythm of our existence."

My brows furrowed. "So… it's one year for one year, one year in heaven or hell for every year here on earth give or take a few?"

"Yes, pretty much a mirror," he said. "The waiting is not punishment. It is preparation. In heaven, those years are spent resting, healing, learning and preparing for the next journey. In hell, if the soul was corrupt, those years are spent facing one's actions, stripped of excuses, feeling the weight of every wrong done to others. Either way, the waiting time equals the years lived."

"That means," I whispered, "you'll be there eighty-some more years before you return?"

He smiled faintly. "Yes. I lived eighty-six years and so my soul will rest, serve and learn in heaven for around eighty-six or so years before I walk the earth again. But those years don't drag as they do here. Time feels different there. Waiting is not empty, it's full."

A shiver ran through me. "Full of what?"

"Full of everything a soul needs," he said softly. "Reflection, healing, worship and service. Like I said, for now, I work with children, others study, others serve in ways you can't imagine, sometimes in other universes or on other planets, even in other galaxies. And when the waiting ends, God places the soul back into this world, in a body chosen for the lessons ahead."

I let that wash over me. My whole life, I had thought of heaven and hell as being final destinations, ending points. The idea that there were pauses in a greater cycle shook me to my core. Now, I knew he was telling me the truth from his own experiences because I knew for a fact that my father wouldn't have believed any of this when he was alive.

"Do we remember?" I asked suddenly. "When we are born again, do we remember any of our past lives?"

His eyes softened with compassion. "Not clearly. Memories would overwhelm the new life. A child could not carry the weight of a past lifetime on its small shoulders. But pieces remain, instincts, gifts, fears, even certain connections. That's why sometimes you meet someone and feel you've known them your whole life, even though you just met. Why certain places feel strangely familiar. The soul remembers more than the mind does."

You mean like a soulmate? "Yes, exactly"

I swallowed, my throat dry. "So all of us, me, you, we've been here before?"

"Many times," he said with certainty. "Each lifetime building upon the last, each live bringing us closer to the fullness that God intended. Think of it like climbing a mountain. You don't reach the peak in one step. You climb, rest, climb again. Sometimes you stumble, sometimes you fall, sometimes you find easier paths. But always, always the goal is the summit, reaching the top."

"And what happens when we reach it?"

"Then the cycle ends," he said with a deep, steady calm. "A soul perfected in love and wisdom no longer needs to be born again. That soul remains in heaven, eternally with God. Some call it eternal salvation. Some call it enlightenment. It's really both."

The thought both thrilled and unsettled me. "And hell? Do those souls get another chance too?"

"Yes," he said firmly. "Remember when I taught you that hell was made for Satan and his fallen angels. It was never intended for humans. Hell is not eternal for most humans. It is a place of reckoning, not annihilation. A murderer, a thief, a soul twisted by cruelty, they must face what they've done, year for year. But when their time is complete, they too are given another chance at life, another chance at salvation. God's justice is perfect, but so is His mercy. No one is cast away in Hell forever unless that's the life they continue to choose.

He kept reminding me over and over that the Bible teaches us that hell was made for Satan and his demons and that it was never intended for humans."

I drew in a long, shaky breath. "That means everyone… even the worst people… they come back?"

"Yes," he said, "though they carry the scars of hell within them. Those scars often become the very lessons they must learn in their next life. A tyrant may return as one oppressed, a thief as one who suffers loss, a cruel person as one who must endure cruelty until they understand. Every life balances the last, until the soul learns God's ultimate love. That is the end of the journey for all souls, to love as God loves us."

I let out a long sigh, my mind reeling. "Dad… that changes everything."

He smiled gently. "That's why I was allowed to come visit you tonight. You've been wrestling with these questions your whole life, feeling the emptiness of death, the injustice of it all. I wanted you to know that nothing is wasted. Not a day. Not a tear. Not one soul."

I pressed my palms against my knees, trying to anchor myself. The room felt both infinite and intimate, like heaven itself had bent low into the living room.

"But Dad," I said quietly, "if we keep coming back… how do we make it matter now? How do I make sure this life isn't wasted?"

He leaned forward, his gaze steady and fierce. "By loving those that God puts into our lives. By choosing good over evil, right over wrong. By listening to the whisper of your soul, that still small voice. Every act of kindness builds for eternity. Every selfish act hinders our eternity. Don't worry about being perfect, only worry about being true, being compassionate, being faithful with what you've been given. That's all God asks."

I nodded slowly, tears welling again.

He reached out once more and though his hand didn't quite touch mine, the warmth of his presence wrapped around me. "Your time here on earth matters, son. Don't ever think it doesn't. Every moment is part of the climb, part of the adventure."

The clock kept ticking, reminding me of time slipping by. Our time together was passing faster than I wanted it to.

But for the first time since his death, I felt less afraid. Because now, I believed there was more, more than just this life as we knew it.

Much more.

The Truth About Hell

I hesitated before asking, afraid of what he might say. “Dad… you’ve told me about heaven. You’ve shown me its beauty, its joy, its light. But tell me more about hell? Have you ever seen it? And if you have… can you describe it to me?”

His smile faded into solemnity and the glow around him dimmed, though it never disappeared. He folded his hands, his eyes heavy with memory.

“Yes, son,” he said slowly. “I have seen it. Not because I wanted to, but because in heaven, truth is given. To understand love fully, you must understand what it looks like when love is rejected. Heaven showed me a glimpse of hell, not to frighten me, but to teach me. And what I saw will stay with me forever.”

I leaned forward, bracing myself.

“Hell is not fire and flames as many imagine,” he said. “It is far worse. It is the absence of light. It’s pitch black; it’s the absence of God’s presence. Imagine walking into a room where the air itself even feels heavy with sorrow. That is the atmosphere of hell. Darkness covers everything, not like the peaceful rest of night, but like smoke that suffocates, pressing down on the soul."

He paused, his eyes distant. "There is no color there. Everything is dark, muted, lifeless. The ground itself is barren, cracked, as though joy has actually been drained from the ground. The air feels thick, hot and humid, carrying the weight of regret and despair. And the silence, oh, the silence is thick and heavy. Not stillness, but emptiness. Sometimes you will hear cries echo in the distance, but even those fade quickly into the vast void. It is not a place of noise, but a place of hollow echoes. It's a place of sorrow and despair, the feeling of fear and complete emptiness."

A shiver ran through me.

"What about the people?" I whispered.

His face grew sorrowful. "Yes, they are there. Souls, countless souls. But they do not walk as we do in heaven. They are bent, burdened, weighed down by the truth of their own sinful lives. Each one carries the full weight of what they did on earth. A murderer feels the pain of every life they ended. A thief feels the loss of everyone they stole from. A liar is trapped in the very web they spun. They are not punished from outside, they are consumed by the truth from within."

I swallowed hard, my throat dry.

"They do not interact as you might think," he continued. "They are aware of each other around them, but there is no fellowship. No friendships, no comfort. Each is isolated in their own reckoning. They may stand next to each other, side by side, but their torment is inward, unique to their own choices. Some rage, some wail, some fall silent with shame. But none escape the horror of truth."

I found my voice again. "How long do they stay there?"

"The same span as their earthly life," he said firmly. "If a man lived fifty years in cruelty, he spends fifty years in hell, facing it. If a woman lived seventy years in selfishness, she spends seventy years reckoning. Not a moment more, not a moment less. Justice is balanced, year for year."

I shook my head slowly, trying to take it in.

"What else did you see there?" I asked softly.

He drew in a deep breath. "The landscape is barren. There are no rivers of life, no gardens, no music. Instead, there are endless plains of dry dust and cold stone. The ground cracks beneath your feet. The air is stale, humid and heavy, almost choking. Shadows move, but they are not alive, just the echoes of souls replaying their deeds. It is a land without beauty, without rest. Even the horizon feels empty, like a void stretching forever."

He paused, his voice lowering. "And yet, it is not chaos. It is ordered. Each soul walks through their years of truth with precision. The place itself seems built for reflection, for correction. Every detail presses the soul to face what it has been."

"And God?" I asked quietly. "Is He there?"

My father shook his head, sorrow etched in his features. “No. That is the greatest torment of all. In heaven, God’s presence is everywhere. In hell, His absence is absolute. Souls thirst for Him but find nothing. They long for even a glimpse of light, but none comes. That emptiness is deeper than pain, deeper than fire. Its longing is unfulfilled.”

He leaned forward, his voice grave. “That is why the soul breaks there. Not just because of the weight of truth, but because of the silence of God. And yet, even in that silence, His mercy waits. When their time is complete, when their reckoning is finished, they are given another life. Another chance to be born again.”

“So it’s not forever?” I asked again, desperate for clarity.

“No,” he said, shaking his head. “Not for most. Hell is not eternal torture. It is a furnace of truth. It strips away lies, pride and cruelty. When the soul emerges, it is scarred, humbled, but ready. Ready to learn, to walk again, to try again. Only a few cling so tightly to hatred that they choose darkness forever. But most… most endure and then they return."

His eyes grew softer. "Think of it as bitter medicine. No one wants it, but it heals. Hell is terrible, but it is not hopeless. God does not abandon His creation, not even there. He allows them to face their deeds, to feel what they caused, so that in the next life, hopefully they can choose love over evil."

He fell silent for a moment, the glow around him brightening again, as though heaven itself pushed back the shadows of his description.

"So, son," he said gently, "don't take hell lightly. It is a real place and it is terrible. But don't let fear rule you, either. Live in love and you need not taste its sorrow. And when you look at others, remember, every soul is still on its journey. The one who stumbles today may rise tomorrow. The one who wanders in darkness may one day shine with light. Never judge a soul as finished. God's work is never finished."

I sat there trembling, shaken by his words. Heaven sounded like home. Hell sounded well, like hell. And together, they painted a picture of eternity more vast and mysterious than I had ever imagined.

A Closer Look at Hell

The air in the room shifted when my father spoke the word "hell." Though the golden glow still wrapped around him, a weight settled into the silence, sobering me. I leaned forward, my hands clasped tightly, bracing myself.

"Son," my father said quietly, "you've seen how people speak of hell on earth. Some laugh at it, treating it like a myth. Others twist it into a weapon, using fear to control. But I want you to know the truth. Hell is real, but it is not what most people think."

I swallowed, my throat dry. "Please, I want to know more."

He drew in a breath, his expression grave yet calm. "Hell is not fire and pitchforks, nor a place where demons dance over tortured souls. It is not eternal torment for most. It is a place of truth. In hell, there are no masks, no excuses. A soul sees itself fully, every action, every cruelty, every selfish act laid bare. There is no hiding, no pretending. You feel the full weight of what you have done to others, the sorrow, the grief, the regret. It's you and you alone, darkness, no fellowship, no worship, no singing or dancing. It's just total loneliness apart from God. That is hell."

The words kept hitting me like stones. I pictured standing in such a place, forced to see every wrong I had ever done, every careless word, every selfish moment. Just total darkness and loneliness. My stomach tightened.

"But why?" I whispered.

"Because God's justice must be served," he said. "Every act of love echoes into eternity, but so does every act of harm. Heaven is mercy; hell is balance. A murderer must feel the pain of every life they ended. A thief must feel the loss they inflicted. A liar must feel the web of betrayal they spun. And they feel it not as punishment from outside, but from within their very soul. That is why it is torment, because the soul itself finally recognizes the depth of its wrongs."

A chill ran through me. "And how long… how long do they stay there?"

He looked at me with steady eyes. "The same as in heaven, the length of their earthly life. Year for year. A man who lived fifty years in cruelty and sin will spend fifty years in hell, stripped of illusions, only facing truth. A woman who lived seventy years in selfishness will spend seventy years in total darkness. The balance is perfect. No more, no less."

I closed my eyes, letting the weight of that sink in. "So… everyone who goes there eventually comes out?"

"Yes," he said firmly. "Hell is not forever, remember, I told you that Hell was made for Satan and his followers, not for humans. There are a few who will choose darkness eternally, who reject love so completely that their souls disintegrate into nothingness. But for most, hell is a furnace that purifies. It burns away the lies, the pride, the cruelty, until the soul is ready to live again, to try again. Hell is terrible, yes. But it is not total hopelessness."

His words sent a strange relief through me, though my chest still felt heavy. "So even the worst people… even murderers…"

"Yes," he said. "Even they. Their time in hell is very painful with much agony and regret, because they are forced to feel what they inflicted. But when the years are complete, they are given another life, another chance to learn, to change, to choose differently, to seek out the Father here on earth. God's justice is unyielding, but His mercy never ends. The cycle is meant to heal, not to destroy."

I stared at him, shaking my head slowly. "That's so different from what we were taught growing up. They always said hell was forever. Eternal."

His gaze softened. "That teaching came from fear, son. From men who misunderstood or who wanted control. Fear can frighten people into obedience, but it cannot teach love. And love is the only thing that lasts. God is love. How could love create eternal torment for every sinner? No, love creates correction, balance, opportunity. Even hell serves love's purpose. Remember how I had to spank you as a child? I still loved you, but as your father, I still needed to discipline you. I did it out of love."

The warmth of his words wrapped around me, though the weight of them pressed deep. “What is it like there?” I asked, my voice almost a whisper.

He paused, his eyes lowering for a moment. When he spoke, his voice carried a sorrowful gravity. “Very dark. Very, very heavy. There is no light, no laughter, no peace. Souls there are consumed with their own guilt. They relive their wrongs, not once but constantly. Time feels long, there are no days, no months and no years. Just darkness stretched by regret and fear. There are no distractions, only truth. And that truth crushes until it breaks the pride of even the hardest of hearts.”

A shiver ran through me. “That sounds unbearable.”

“It is,” he said softly. “That is why it changes people. A man who laughed at his cruelty on earth cannot laugh in hell. A thief who felt no shame cannot deny the anguish of those he stole from. A liar cannot escape the mirror of his own words. Hell is unbearable, but it is also what makes the soul ready to change.”

I stared at the floor, my mind reeling. "So heaven and hell are both part of the cycle. Two classrooms, like you said."

"Exactly," he said with a nod. "One teaches joy, the other teaches truth. Together, they prepare souls for rebirth. Heaven heals; hell humbles and both lead to growth."

I looked up at him, tears burning my eyes again. "Dad… do you know people who went there? People we knew?"

He nodded slowly, his face solemn. "Yes, some friends from High School. Some of our neighbors we both knew. Even some in our distant relatives. Souls I loved, souls I grew up with. It grieved me, but I understood. They must face what they had done. And though I cannot reach them while they are there, I know they will one day emerge, broken but ready to learn again. That gives me peace."

The clock ticked again, a reminder that our time was slipping away. I wanted to ask a thousand more questions, but my father's gaze told me he was choosing each word carefully, knowing they had to last me a lifetime.

"Listen to me, son," he said, his voice steady. "Hell is real, but you don't have to fear it if you walk in faith with Jesus Christ. Remember that Jesus paid the price for our sins on the cross. When we choose to live for Christ every choice of kindness, every act of compassion, every good deed keeps you away from Hell. Continue to live in faith. Forgive quickly. Love deeply. Stay close to Jesus to the very end, don't ever give up running the race. That is how you avoid the darkness."

I nodded, my throat tight.

"And remember this too," he added, his eyes fierce now. "Never judge too harshly. The man you see as wicked today may one day turn his life over to Christ. Every soul is still on its journey. Trust God's justice. Trust His mercy."

His words settled into me like seeds, sharp but life-giving. I knew I would carry them always.

He leaned back slightly, the glow around him pulsing gently. "Now you understand the balance. Heaven for healing, hell for truth. Both real. Both necessary. Both temporary and both under the hand of a God who loves perfectly."

The heaviness in the room eased slightly, replaced by a strange, quiet peace.

And I knew I would never see heaven and hell the same way again.

A Glimpse into Eternity

For a few long moments, neither of us spoke. His words about hell lingered like the echo of a storm, sobering yet strangely clarifying. The golden glow around him remained steady and I realized that while the weight of truth was heavy, it was not without hope. That everyone has the opportunity at some point in their lives to accept God's plan of Salvation.

Finally, I broke the silence. "So heaven heals us. Hell humbles us. And then... we come back. But why, Dad? Why not just stay in heaven once we get there? Why return at all?"

"That's the question every soul asks at some point. Why return to the pain, the struggle, the uncertainty of earth? The answer is simple, though living it feels anything but: because earth is the only place where free will and our choice can truly grow. We don't have free will in Heaven because God is there, you can't help but feel His glory. But on earth, everyone has to make their own choice."

"Choice," I repeated.

"Yes. In heaven, God's love surrounds you. In hell, truth presses upon you. But only on earth you choose. You choose whether to love or hate, to forgive or to hold grudges, to be generous or greedy. Earth is the proving ground. It is where the soul becomes what it will ultimately be. It's part of the test to see if we fail or not, if we choose to please God or ourselves."

I sat back slowly, thinking about the thousands of choices I had made in just the past week. Most of them small. Some I regretted. Some I barely remembered. Yet he was telling me that every single one mattered.

He leaned forward, his voice calm but steady. "Son, eternity is not about sitting still. It's about growing closer and closer to the likeness of God. Every life is a step on that journey. Each life teaches us something new. That's why reincarnation exists, not to punish, but to give the soul chance after chance to learn love fully. That's why we are born again and again until we are made perfect in God's image."

"But dad, the earth doesn't seem to be getting better but only worse. It seems that there is more evil now than there was 50 or even 100 years ago."

"Yes, it seems that way, doesn't it? But the reality is that we are coming to the end of time."

You mean like Revelations?

"Exactly, and many of the righteous, Godly souls that were once here and have now returned to heaven are not returning like they used to in the past. It's all part of God's master plan."

My chest ached. "But it seems so slow… so long. Lifetime after lifetime. Years waiting in heaven or in hell. Why not make it shorter?"

He chuckled softly, the familiar sound of his humor even in the midst of profound truths.

"Because the soul is not in a hurry, even if we are. God's time is not our time. Each lesson must take root deeply or it will not last. Think of a tree, son. You can't rush its growth. If you try, you weaken it or even kill it. The roots must spread slowly, the trunk must thicken with the seasons. So it is with our soul. Slow growth is lasting growth."

I breathed out slowly, his words settling over me like gentle rain.

He continued, "When a soul has learned enough, when it has chosen God's love consistently across many lives, then the cycle ends. That soul no longer needs earth. It remains in heaven, complete, whole, forever with God for eternity. Some call that salvation, some call it enlightenment, some call it perfection. But it is all the same: the soul finally becoming what it was always meant to be, one with God."

A lump formed in my throat. "And you... you're still on that journey, too?"

He nodded, no shame in his eyes. "Yes. I still have lessons to learn. My eighty-six years on earth taught me much, but I am not finished yet. That is why I serve children in heaven now, it prepares me for what comes next. Each role shapes the soul further. Even now, I am still becoming."

His humility touched me deeply. In life, my father had been wise, respected, and a man many looked up to. Yet here he was, admitting freely that he was still learning. That eternity itself had now become his classroom.

"Does it ever get discouraging?" I asked.

He shook his head. "Not in heaven. There is no discouragement there, only purpose. Souls understand that every step matters, even the hard ones. On earth, you feel frustration because you cannot see the whole picture. But in heaven, you get a better glimpse of it and that glimpse is enough to keep you moving with purpose and with peace."

I sat quietly, letting the idea settle. The thought that my life now was one rung on a great ladder of existence both overwhelmed and comforted me.

"Dad," I said after a moment, "what about people we love? Families, friends? If everyone is born again at different times, are we ever really together?"

He smiled gently. "Yes. In heaven, those bonds are never lost. Souls recognize each other beyond the veil of earthly memory. Families find one another, again and again. Sometimes on earth, they even return together. That's why certain families feel bound by something deeper than chance. That's why some friends feel like brothers, some spouses feel destined. Souls weave together across lifetimes, finding each other again and again until the lessons of God's love are complete."

My chest tightened, this time with a strange warmth. "So we'll see each other again?"

"Many times," he said, his eyes glowing. "On earth, in heaven, across lifetimes, you and I are bound in love. Love never dies. It only transforms. You might be my son in this life but I might be your big brother in my next life."

Tears blurred my vision and I wiped them quickly. "I needed to hear that," I thought to myself.

He leaned closer, his gaze steady. "Then carry it with you. Every time you feel alone, remember: love binds us across all eternity. Even when we are in different worlds, we are never far apart. I can still hear you whenever you think of me. Don't be afraid to call out my name."

The golden glow brightened for a moment, as if emphasizing his words.

"And remember this too," he added. "Eternity is not just a faraway thing. It begins now. Every choice you make is shaping your eternity. Every act of kindness, every word of love, it all matters, more than you will ever know. When you live with eternity in mind, even the smallest act becomes sacred."

I nodded slowly, my heart heavy yet lifted.

"So heaven, hell and earth are all part of God's master plan," I said quietly. "Steps taken in the same journey?"

"Exactly," he said. "Three classrooms of the same school. Earth for choice. Heaven for healing. Hell for truth. And beyond them, eternity with God our Father, when the soul has finally learned to love without flaw."

I drew in a shaky breath, realizing how much my view of life and death had changed in the span of minutes.

“Dad,” I whispered, “this is more than I can take in right now.”

He chuckled softly, a familiar sound that steadied me. “It’s alright son. You don’t need to understand it all tonight. Just carry the seeds. They’ll grow in time.”

The grandfather clock in the living room ticked again, louder now in my ears and I realized with a pang that our time was running shorter. Yet even that thought didn’t crush me as before. Because now, I knew that our time was not the end. Not for him, not for me, not for anyone. But a beginning of truth and understanding about what lies ahead for all of us.

He leaned back, his expression peaceful. “That’s the glimpse I wanted to give you, son. Eternity is bigger than fear, bigger than sorrow, bigger than death. It is love unfolding, again and again, until every soul is whole.”

And in that moment, I believed him.

The Personal Connection

The glow around him softened, as though heaven itself was leaning closer to listen. My father shifted in the chair, resting his hands together and gave me a look I remembered from countless late-night talks when I was younger. It was the look he wore when he wanted me to pay attention, not as a child, but this time as a grown man.

"I've told you about heaven and I've explained about hell, about being reincarnated and born again and how eternity works," he said, his voice quieter now, more personal. "But I want to speak to you not just as a messenger from beyond, but as your father. I want you to know what I've learned, not just as a soul, but as your father, the man you have known your whole life."

I swallowed hard, my chest tightening at the sound of his voice.

He leaned forward, his eyes steady on mine. "When I left this earth, I looked back over eighty-six years. And son, do you know what mattered most in the end?"

I shook my head, though the answer seemed to rise inside me already.

"Love," he said simply. "Not the titles, not the money, not the houses not the winning or the losing. Love! Who I gave it to, who I withheld it from, who I forgave and who I didn't forgive. That's what weighed on me most in those first days beyond."

His words struck me hard. I thought of the times I had held grudges, the words I had left unsaid, the people I had let drift away.

He continued, his voice carrying the weight of honesty. "There are things I regret. Times I worked too much and listened too little. Times I let my temper speak louder than my patience. Times I thought I was strong when really, I was just stubborn. But in heaven, regret doesn't chain you, it teaches you. And I've learned this: if you still have breath in your lungs, it's not too late to love others more."

Tears blurred my vision. “Dad, you did love us. You weren’t perfect, but you did love us.”

He smiled softly. “I did, I wasn’t perfect but I did with all I knew how. But now I see God’s love even more clearly. It’s more than feelings, it’s choosing kindness when it’s inconvenient. It’s giving grace when someone doesn’t deserve it. It’s being present when it would be easier to turn away. That’s what I wish I had done more. It’s living as Christ lived. He is our example to live by.”

His words pierced me, not as condemnation, but as a gift, a warning, a guide, a compass.

“You still can,” he added gently. “You still have many years ahead of you. Don’t waste them. Don’t put off forgiveness, don’t delay compassion, don’t wait for the perfect moment to say the words that matter for eternity. Life is shorter than you think and eternity is longer than you can imagine. Choose Christs love now, while you have the chance.”

I pressed a hand to my face, trying to steady my breath. “Dad… I’m afraid sometimes. Afraid I’ll waste my life. Afraid I won’t do enough.”

His voice softened, carrying the same reassurance he had given me as a boy after a bad dream. “You don’t have to do *enough*, son. You just have to do *what God has given you to do*. God doesn’t measure you by someone elses path. He measures you by faithfulness, by whether you walked the road given to you. Don’t compare, don’t compete. Just be faithful with what God has given you. Remember that Jesus has paid the price, as long as you live for Him, everything will be okay!”

His words sank deep, loosening a knot in my throat I hadn’t noticed was there.

“And don’t be afraid of failing,” he added. “Failure isn’t final, not in God’s eyes. It’s just another lesson, another chance to grow. Even when you stumble, you’re still moving forward if you get back up. Eternity doesn’t demand perfection. it invites persistence.”

I let out a shaky laugh through the tears. "You always knew how to talk me off a ledge."

He chuckled softly. "Well, some things don't change."

The clock ticked again and I felt the weight of time pressing in. I didn't want it to end, at least not yet. There were still so many things I wanted to ask, so many words I wanted to hear.

"Dad," I said quickly, "what about you? What are you doing now? You said you are working with children… what's that like for you?"

A light returned to his eyes, the kind of brightness I remembered when he used to teach children at Good News Clubs, 5 Day Clubs and at Camp Good News. "It's a joy, pure joy. Children are so eager to hear more Bible stories, they even ask me about you kids. I tell them how you worked with Jr. Hi kids for so many years, about your summer servants program where you lead so many kids to Christ. It brings them closer to God's heart when they hear these stories than you would actually realize. They carry innocence, even when earth cuts their lives short. In heaven, I help them grow, teach them truth, and surround them with love. It's like being part of an eternal school of laughter and wonder. I never tire of it."

He paused, then added softly, "It feels like my purpose followed me here. That comforts me. I didn't lose myself when I died, I found more of myself."

His words filled me with an odd mixture of joy and longing. I could almost picture him surrounded by children as they sat there and listened to him tell stories about Jesus, his family, and the Old Testament Prophets that he used to teach here on earth. I could see his face lit up with delight. It was easy to believe that was exactly where he belonged, where Gold wanted him to be.

He looked at me again, his voice lowering. "But my greatest joy is knowing you're still living your life for Christ, still working out your salvation, still with time to love and make sacrifices for the kingdom. That's why I was given this time to come visit you. Not for me, but for you. To remind you that life is precious and death is not the end.

To tell you that I'm proud of you, even when you doubt yourself. To tell you that I believe in you, even when you don't. I'm so proud of you for writing the devotional workbooks "52 Weeks Through the New Testament."

The tears spilled freely now. "Dad… I had no idea that you knew that I made a devotional workbook for New Believers called "52 Weeks through the New Testament." I so needed to hear that more than anything."

He leaned forward, his face close to mine, his eyes fierce with fatherly love. "I am always there with you, watching over you and your kids, my grandkids as well, let that sink in deep, son. Remember to carry it like a stone in your pocket. Whenever you feel lost, remember: your father is watching over you and God is too."

I nodded, unable to speak, my throat was tight. I just realized that dad reminded me when we were campers at Camp Good News up in the Big Bear mountains in California. How he told us campers to pick up a small rock and keep it in our pocket for as long as we could as a way to remind us of the commitment we had just made to follow Jesus Christ and to live our lives daily for Him. I think I kept mine in my pocket for a couple of months until I lost it in the washing machine.

The glow around him pulsed again, brighter now, as if reminding me that our time was slipping fast.

He smiled gently. “I don’t know how much time together we have left. But if this is the last thing I get to say, let it be this: live with love, walk with faith in Jesus Christ and don’t be afraid. Death cannot end what God has begun in you. And one day, when your journey is complete, I’ll be there waiting to meet you. Until then, just keep climbing.”

I closed my eyes, letting his words wash over me, branding themselves into my heart.

When I opened them again, he was still there but it looked like Jesus was standing there right behind him, but the glow seemed more intense now, as though the thread holding him to this world was beginning to fray. I knew our farewell was coming soon.

The Farewell

The glow around my father shimmered like a flame in the wind, still steady but thinner now, as though Jesus' hand was gently drawing him back. He glanced at the grandfather clock and smiled wryly.

"Time," he said, "Even when borrowed from heaven, is still time. It slips faster than we want."

My heart clenched. "No. Not yet. Please, don't go, not yet."

He leaned forward, his eyes loving, his voice steady. "Our time together was a gift, son. Enough to speak what needed to be said, enough to plant seeds that will grow long after I go. I can't stay longer, not without tearing the veil between heaven and earth. And that veil must remain."

The tears welled again, hot and unrelenting. "I'm not ready to let you go a second time dad."

He gave a small, knowing smile. "You don't have to be ready. No one ever is. But you can be willing. Willing to let go, because you know I am not lost. Willing to live fully, knowing death is only a doorway into eternity, not a wall."

I shook my head, my voice trembling. "It doesn't feel like a doorway. It feels like a thief. It stole you from me again."

His eyes softened, the golden glow reflecting in them. "Death feels like theft because love is real. You ache because you loved me and I ache, too. But eternity proves the thief has no power. It cannot keep us apart. Love is always stronger."

He rose slowly from his favorite chair, the glow around him brightening for a moment. He stood tall, more vibrant than I had ever remembered him in life, as though heaven had restored what time had worn away.

"Come," he said gently.

I stood, hesitant, my legs trembling.

He extended his hand, not quite touching mine, but close enough to feel that warmth that pulsed between us. "You may not feel the grasp of my fingers, but you can feel the truth. This is not goodbye. It is only 'until later.'"

The tears blurred everything. “Dad, I don’t want you to go.”

“I know,” he whispered. “But listen to me, son. Carry what you’ve been taught your whole life and especially what I’ve told you tonight. Heaven is real and so is hell. The soul continues, learning through lifetimes, until God’s love inside of us is perfected. That’s the truth I came to give you. But more than that, carry the truth of my love. That will never fade.” I nodded, unable to form words.

He looked at me one last time, his expression glowing with pride. “You’ve done better than you think. You’ve been stronger than you know. And you will go further than you can imagine. Don’t forget that. I will always believe in you. Always!”

The glow surged and I knew our time was almost gone. “Dad!” I cried out in desperation.

He smiled, and for a heartbeat, I saw both the father I knew and something greater, his soul, whole and eternal. “I’ll see you again, son. In another lifetime, in heaven or both. Until then, live with courage. Live with love, trust in Christ Jesus our Lord and Savior."

And then, he was gone.

The golden light faded like morning mist under the sun, leaving only the lamp's dim glow in the corner of the room. The air felt empty, heavy with silence. I stood there, frozen, my heart aching as though it had been cracked open and filled with fire.

He was gone, but was he?

The memory of his words, his presence, clung to me like a second skin. My tears flowed freely, but beneath them was something else, peace. A peace I hadn't felt in the year since he had been gone.

His favorite grandfather clock ticked on. The world moved. And I breathed, carrying him inside me.

Reflection

It has been months since that night, yet I still feel the echo of his presence. Sometimes, when I close my eyes, I can hear his voice, calm and steady, reminding me that God's love is stronger than death.

I know people will say it was just a dream, a grief-born vision, the desperate mind of a son aching for his father. Maybe they're right, maybe they're wrong? But I know what I felt. I know what I saw and I know what I heard. I know what changed inside me.

My father came for approximately fifteen minutes, heaven came down and I was able to see him again. He told me of heaven, a place of joy, learning and love. He told me of hell, the darkness, the complete void and the self-torment and that it's the truth that purifies. He told me what it meant to truly be born again, of the soul's long journey toward endless love. And he told me of his own life, his regrets and his hopes for me.

Most of all, he told me he believed in me.

That is the gift I get to carry for the rest of my life. When fear rises, when regret claws, when I wonder if I actually matter, I remember his words: *"Your father believes in you and God does too."*

Approximately fifteen minutes, that's all I had. But it was enough. Enough to see beyond the veil, enough to turn grief into hope, enough to remind me that death is not the end but its only the beginning.

Someday, I know that I will see him again. Perhaps in heaven, perhaps in another lifetime, perhaps both. But until then, I will live and I will love. I will climb the mountain, step by step, until my soul, too, is made whole and is made complete in Christ.

And when that day comes, when the cycle is complete, I know what I'll hear my Father say:

"Well done, my good and faithful servant. Welcome home."

So, is this *"The End"* or is it just the beginning?

The Romans Road to Salvation

Our Need for Salvation Romans 3:23 "For all have sinned and fall short of the glory of God." Every person is separated from God because of sin. Sin isn't just "big wrongs" but anything that falls short of God's holiness.

The Consequence of Sin Romans 6:23a "For the wages of sin is death…" Sin earns a penalty, spiritual death and separation from God.

God's Gift of Life Romans 6:23b "…but the gift of God is eternal life in Christ Jesus our Lord." Unlike wages, gifts are freely given, not earned. Salvation is a gift we simply receive.

God's Love Demonstrated Romans 5:8 "But God demonstrates His own love for us in this: While we were still sinners, Christ died for us." God showed His love by sending Jesus to die in our place.

Our Response Romans 10:9&10 "If you declare with your mouth, 'Jesus is Lord,' and believe in your heart that God raised him from the dead, you will be saved." Salvation comes by believing and confessing Christ as Lord.

Assurance of Salvation Romans 10:13 "For everyone who calls on the name of the Lord will be saved." God's promise is clear: if you call on Him sincerely, you will be saved.

Would you like to pray this simple prayer and accept Jesus Christ as your personal Lord and Savior today?

Prayer: "Lord Jesus, I know that I am a sinner and I need Your forgiveness. I believe You died on the cross for my sins and rose from the dead on the third day. I turn from my sin and invite You into my life. I confess You as my Lord and Savior. Thank You for saving me. In Jesus name I pray, amen.

Please write your name and today's date below if you just prayed this prayer for the first time.

Name: ______________________________

Date: ______________________________

I would love to pray for you as you begin your journey towards heaven.

Please contact me at:

TomZegan@Hotmail.com
with your name and address, I have something I'd like to send you.

Made in the USA
Coppell, TX
15 February 2026